Cambridge **Discovery Education**™

▶ INTERACTIVE READERS

Series editor: Bob Hastings

GROWING UP
FROM BABY TO ADULT

A1⁺

Nic Harris and Diane Naughton

CAMBRIDGE
UNIVERSITY PRESS

University Printing House, Cambridge CB2 8BS, United Kingdom

One Liberty Plaza, 20th Floor, New York, NY 10006, USA

477 Williamstown Road, Port Melbourne, VIC 3207, Australia

4843/24, 2nd Floor, Ansari Road, Daryaganj, Delhi – 110002, India

79 Anson Road, #06–04/06, Singapore 079906

Cambridge University Press is part of the University of Cambridge.

It furthers the University's mission by disseminating knowledge in the pursuit of education, learning and research at the highest international levels of excellence.

www.cambridge.org
Information on this title: www.cambridge.org/9781107687448

First published 2014
20 19 18 17 16 15 14 13 12 11 10 9 8 7 6 5 4

Printed in Dubai by Oriental Press

A catalogue record for this publication is available from the British Library

Library of Congress Cataloging in Publication Data

Harris, Nicholas, 1956-
    Growing up : from baby to adult / Nic Harris and Diane Naughton.
      pages cm. — (Cambridge discovery interactive readers)
    ISBN 978-1-107-68744-8 (pbk. : alk. paper)
1. Human growth—Juvenile literature. 2. English language—Textbooks for foreign speakers.
3. Readers (Elementary) I. Title.

QP84.H29 2013
612.6—dc23

                                  2013025127

ISBN 978-1-107-68744-8

Additional resources for this publication at www.cambridge.org

Layout services, art direction, book design, and photo research: Q2ABillSMITH GROUP
Editorial services: Hyphen S.A.
Audio production: CityVox, New York
Video production: Q2ABillSMITH GROUP

Contents

Before You Read:
Get Ready!

Every animal grows up, but each kind of animal does it differently. Read on to learn all about growing up!

Words to Know

Look at the pictures. Then complete the definitions below with the correct words.

elephant

lion

snake

adult female

adult male

teenager

Animals

❶ _____ : a long, thin animal with no legs

❷ _____ : a very big, gray animal with a long nose

❸ _____ : an animal from the cat family

Humans

❹ _____ : a woman who stopped growing

❺ _____ : someone 13–19 years old

❻ _____ : a man who stopped growing

Words to Know

Read the text. Then complete the sentences below with the correct highlighted words.

Human parents look after their babies after they are born. They give them food, warm clothes, and a safe place to live. Many animal parents look after their babies also, but some animals don't do anything to help their babies.

With time, all babies grow up and get stronger. When they are old enough, they can leave their parents. They become adults. But growing up is not always easy! There are many dangerous things in life. For humans, it can be dangerous to drive a car or do some sports. For animals, there are bigger animals that want to eat them.

1 Is the water warm _____ to swim? Yes, it is.

2 Don't play with that knife. That's _____!

3 We _____ John's dog when he goes on vacation.

4 Most babies in the USA are _____ in hospitals.

5 After college, some students _____ doctors or teachers.

6 When these little brown birds _____, they will be beautiful swans.

? PREDICT

Think about the animals you know. Do they look after their babies? What do they do for them?

A swan and her babies

A baby alligator

CHAPTER 1

The Start of Life

HOW DOES LIFE START? IS IT THE SAME FOR PEOPLE AND ANIMALS?

Some animals, like birds and alligators, start life inside an egg. But many animals carry their babies in their bodies.

For the first nine months before humans are born, they grow inside their mothers. Baby cats are inside their mothers for only two months. A female lion carries her baby for about four months. And an elephant is inside its mother for 22 months.

The mother is usually the most important parent. The baby is safe inside her. It takes food from her. The mother often looks after the baby after it is born, too.

But sometimes the father is more important. For example, the female seahorse puts as many as 1,500 eggs in the male seahorse's body. The father then carries the eggs for two to four weeks. The eggs get food from his body until they **hatch**. Now the baby seahorse can look after itself. Dad's job is finished!

The seahorse dad is so important!

The male sea catfish is important, too. After the female puts her eggs on the sea floor, the male takes them in his mouth. And they stay there for about two months. Then, the eggs hatch, and the baby fish swim out to start their lives.

Eggs are safe in a catfish dad's mouth.

Video Quest

Kittens

Watch the video about kittens. What does the mother cat want to do? What problem does she have?

CHAPTER 2

Babies

ALL BABIES NEED THEIR PARENTS TO LOOK AFTER THEM. OR DO THEY?

Most new baby sharks can swim and look for food. But great white shark babies start finding food for themselves before they are born. They hatch out of eggs inside the mother and get hungry. They eat other eggs, and sometimes they eat their brothers and sisters!

Adult snakes don't look after their babies. Snakes look after themselves from day one. The African black mamba is one of the world's most dangerous snakes. A baby black mamba is as dangerous as an adult. It can catch and eat small animals as soon as it hatches.

A zebra with her baby

Baby kangaroos live in pouches.

A zebra baby can walk about 15 minutes after it's born. After one hour, it can run. This is very important. Lions love to eat baby zebras. But baby zebras can run and stay near their mother and the other adult zebras. Then they are safer.

Other animals can do very little when they are born. The kangaroo is born after only 35 days inside its mother. The baby is very small: two centimeters long. That's smaller than your eye! It climbs into its mother's pouch to be safe, and it stays there for 7 to 10 months!

Video Quest

Baby Animals

Watch the video to learn about different baby animals. What is coming out of the egg? How old is the baby elephant?

Are you my mommy?

Baby birds can't fly, and their parents bring them food every day. When they grow, they start trying to fly. Sometimes the mother helps. She stands near the nest[1] with some food. The small birds try to get the food, but they often fall to the **ground**. After many accidents, they learn to fly.

Many baby animals really need their parents. So what if their parents die? Many adult animals look after the babies of another animal of the same kind. But dogs sometimes look after other kinds of animals, like kittens, baby chickens,[2] or even baby tigers.

[1]**nest:** a home that birds make, often in trees
[2]**chickens:** birds we find on a farm. We eat their meat and eggs.

And what about us? There are about 370,000 human babies born every day somewhere in the world. Babies can't walk, talk, or see very well. (Some people think babies are good swimmers, but this isn't right. If you put them in water, they move their arms and legs, but they aren't really swimming.) A human baby dies very quickly if its parents or other adults don't look after it.

In the first two years, babies learn many things. At 8 to 12 months, they usually say their first word. Between 9 and 18 months, they start walking. But they're not like zebras. They will need the help of adults for many years to come!

? APPLY

Children learn many things very quickly. Think of the children you know. At what age did they learn to draw, read, write, or use a computer?

CHAPTER 3

Adolescence

ADOLESCENCE IS A DIFFICULT TIME, BUT WHY?

Let's look at humans first. Between the ages of 10 and 17, girls usually grow about 23 centimeters and boys about 38 centimeters. Girls usually get heavier by about 17 kilograms and boys by about 24 kilograms.

Teenagers can grow very quickly in a short time. This is called a growth spurt. In a growth spurt, a teenager can grow more than 12 centimeters in one year. In girls, these growth spurts start earlier than in boys. This is why girls of 12 are often taller than boys of the same age.

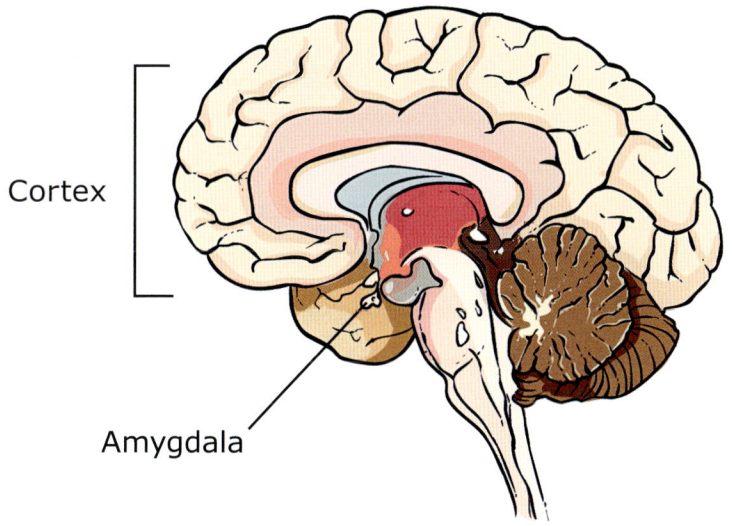

Cortex

Amygdala

And what about inside their heads? Do teenagers think differently from adults?

One part of the brain is called the amygdala. This makes us feel angry, happy, or sad. Another part of the brain, called the cortex, helps us make good **decisions**.

In **adolescents**, the cortex is small, so they use the amygdala much more. Teenagers often get angry or sad very quickly. They often don't make good decisions and do dangerous things. Between the ages of 16 and 19, more people die in accidents than at any other time.

? ANALYZE

What other kinds of problems do teenagers often have at school, with their parents, or with friends? Are these problems because of the changes in their brains?

Most animals start **adolescence** at a younger age than humans. Elephants start adolescence when they stop drinking their mother's milk, usually between 5 and 10 years old. Adolescence usually finishes when they are 17. During adolescence, a male elephant leaves its mother and goes with a group of other young males. But a female elephant stays with her mother.

Male lions start to grow a lot of hair on their heads when they are about 18 months old. This is called a mane. If a lion has a very big mane, it shows that he is a very important lion.

Male lions have a mane.

Puppies love to chew!

Adolescence in cats starts at seven months and ends at 12 months. At this time, female cats start looking for male cats to have babies with. And male cats leave a strong smell[3] in the places where they live. This tells other male cats to stay away!

Dog adolescence is from six months of age. At about the same time, puppies also grow new adult teeth. This makes them feel bad, and they often chew[4] things. This can be a very bad time for you, too, if you have a dog. The second teeth are strong, and puppies chew everything!

[3]**smell:** something we know about because of our nose
[4]**chew:** what you do with your teeth when you are eating something

CHAPTER 4

Becoming an Adult

IT'S TIME TO GROW UP.

People stop growing at different times. So when does adolescence end and **adulthood** begin?

In most countries, you're an adult when you're 18 years old. But in some countries, adulthood starts earlier or later. In Cuba, for example, you're an adult at 16, but in Egypt, you don't become an adult in all ways until you're 21.

Why is this important? Because when you're an adult, you can do many things you couldn't do before. For example, you can vote,[5] **get married**, or drive a car.

In many countries, when somebody becomes an adult, they have a party. But in some parts of the world, people do dangerous things.

[5]**vote:** help choose the people to run your country

On the small South Pacific island of Vanuatu, young men jump from a high place, 30 meters above the ground. They put a long, strong rope around their leg. It stops them from hitting the ground and dying. But it's still dangerous.

In Australia, adolescent Aboriginal boys have to live **alone** for as long as six months in the Australian outback.[6] The young men have to find food and water. It's very hot and dry in the outback and there are dangerous animals, like snakes. In the past, most Aboriginal boys did this, but not many do it now.

In one part of Ethiopia, before a young man can get married, he has to run on top of some cows and not fall down. This shows he is leaving **childhood** behind and starting life as an adult.

[6] **outback:** places in Australia that aren't near any towns or cities

A young Vanuatan man

Aborigines were the first people in Australia.

17

Mentawai women like to have very sharp teeth.

And what about girls? The Mentawai people live in Indonesia. When a young Mentawai girl becomes an adult, her teeth become very important. She wants to make them as sharp as possible. She knows that Mentawai men love sharp teeth.

In Mexico, when a girl is 15, she becomes a woman. There's a big party (a *quinceañera*, in Spanish). People give the girl lots of presents,[7] and everybody has a lot of fun!

[7] **present:** something people give you on your birthday

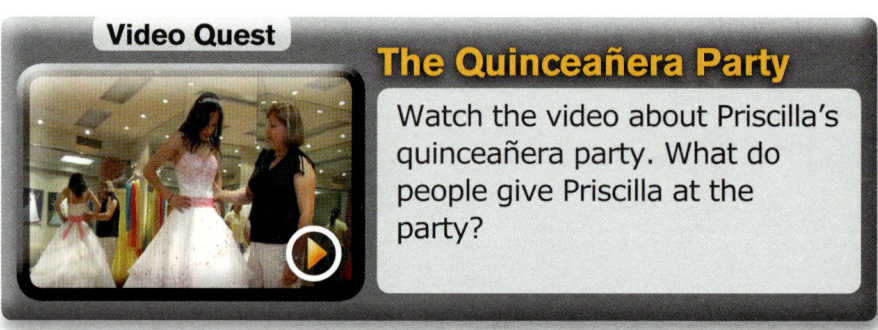

Video Quest

The Quinceañera Party

Watch the video about Priscilla's quinceañera party. What do people give Priscilla at the party?

When some animals become adults, their bodies become very different. For example, an adult frog is very different from a tadpole – a baby frog. A tadpole is born in water. It's like a fish. The tadpole then grows legs and becomes a frog. The adult frog can then leave the water.

And what about butterflies? The mother butterfly puts her eggs on a plant. A caterpillar hatches from the egg and starts to eat the plant. Then, it makes a cocoon, something like a little house. Inside the cocoon, the caterpillar changes. After a few weeks an adult butterfly comes out.

Frogs eat insects, sometimes butterflies.

CHAPTER 5

What Do You Think?

ARE YOU TOO OLD OR TOO YOUNG? WHEN IS THE RIGHT AGE TO DO DIFFERENT THINGS?

Before 1940 in England, many children aged 5 to 14 worked on farms and in factories. In Africa today, about 65 million children work. In Roman times, girls often got married and had children when they became adolescents. But now most people wait until they're much older before they have babies. But what is right? When are we old enough to do things?

Do you agree or disagree with these ideas? Put a check (✓) in the right place. Why do you agree or disagree with each idea?

Idea	Agree	Disagree
A child of 7 can look after a kitten or a small dog.		
It's good for children of 10 to have a cell phone.		
At 13, a teenager can choose when to go to bed.		
It's OK for a 14-year-old to work on a Saturday.		
A 15-year-old can stay out until 11 p.m. on weekends.		
At 15, you're old enough to look after your brothers and sisters.		
Age 16 is too young to get married.		
A good age to learn to drive is 17.		
At 20, people make good decisions.		
Age 45 is too old to have a baby.		
People over 50 can't do some jobs.		
A good age to stop working is 65.		

After You Read

Read the sentences and choose Ⓐ, Ⓑ, or Ⓒ.

1 Human babies grow inside their mothers for less time than baby _____.

  Ⓐ cats

  Ⓑ lions

  Ⓒ elephants

2 Male seahorses _____.

  Ⓐ put eggs on the sea floor

  Ⓑ eat the female's eggs

  Ⓒ look after the female's eggs

3 A baby zebra _____.

  Ⓐ can walk a short time after it's born

  Ⓑ walks as soon as it's born

  Ⓒ walks as fast as an adult zebra

4 When human babies are born, they can't really _____.

  Ⓐ hear

  Ⓑ see

  Ⓒ swim

5 Adolescent girls usually start growing _____.

  Ⓐ earlier than boys

  Ⓑ later than boys

  Ⓒ about the same time as boys

6 Teenagers often _____.

  Ⓐ think like adults

  Ⓑ get angry easily

  Ⓒ have big cortexes

7 In Ethiopia, a young man can't get married until he _____.

    (A) can run over some animals

    (B) is more than 21

    (C) starts working on a farm

8 An adult butterfly _____.

    (A) has very few babies

    (B) becomes a caterpillar

    (C) comes out of a cocoon

Complete the Text

Complete the paragraph with the correct words from the box.

adult	enough	kittens	married
born	growing up	looks after	teenagers

    Jack and Sally have five children, a dog, and a cat. Sally is a doctor, so Jack stays at home and **1** _____ the children. The youngest child, Lily, is a baby. She was **2** _____ in May. Susie is 12, and she is **3** _____ quickly. Paul and John are **4** _____. They're often angry, and they want to stay in bed all day. At 17, Holly is the oldest. She's learning to drive, and she's going to be an **5** _____ soon. She has a boyfriend. She'd like to get **6** _____ one day, but she knows she isn't old **7** _____ now. Life isn't easy for Jack. The dog has six new puppies, and the cat has five new **8** _____. What a house!

Remember

Think of one thing you learned about each animal. How are these animals different from humans?

1 cats: _____

2 birds: _____

3 seahorses: _____

4 elephants: _____

5 snakes: _____

Answer Key

Words to Know, page 4
Animals: **1** snake **2** elephant **3** lion
Humans: **1** adult female **2** teenager **3** adult male

Words to Know, page 5
1 enough **2** dangerous **3** look after **4** born
5 become **6** grow up

Predict, page 5   *Answers will vary.*

Video Quest, page 7
The mother wants to take the kittens to a quieter place,
but they don't want to go.

Video Quest, page 9
A baby alligator is coming out of the egg. The baby
elephant is two years old.

Apply, page 11   *Answers will vary.*

Analyze, page 13   *Answers will vary.*

Video Quest, page 18
People give Priscilla 15 flowers.

Choose the Correct Answers, page 22
1 C **2** C **3** A **4** C **5** A **6** B **7** A **8** C

Complete the Text, page 23
1 looks after **2** born **3** growing up **4** teenagers
5 adult **6** married **7** enough **8** kittens

Remember, page 23   *Answers will vary.*